Socks for Everybody!

BY ALLISON GRIFFITH FOR KNIT PICKS

Copyright 2018 © Knit Picks

All rights reserved. This book or any portion thereof may not be reproduced or used in any manner whatsoever without the express written permission of the publisher except for the use of brief quotations in a book review.

Photography by Amy Setter

Printed in the United States of America

Third Printing, 2020

ISBN 978-1-62767-187-3

Versa Press, Inc
800-447-7829

www.versapress.com

CONTENTS

Introduction	4
Yarn & Needles	7
Notions	9
Gauge & Sizing	11
Math Time!	13
Top Down Instructions	15
Toe Up Instructions	21
Finishing	27
Cuff, Toe, & Heel Library	29
Stitch Pattern Library	32
Tutorials	39
Notes	61
Sock Size Chart & Abbreviations	63

INTRODUCTION

I didn't always love making socks. In fact, I was terrified of them for years. They seemed confusing, complicated, and they were knit at an impossibly small gauge. And don't even get me started on short rows! (Shudder!)

It took me a good decade of knitting before I could muster the courage to give them a try. I took a trip to my local yarn store, picked out a pattern, a set of teeny needles, and skein of a mysterious purple wool blend from the clearance bin. I was so excited to start knitting! I made it through the cuff and halfway through the heel before I decided it was too hard and gave up. That half-sock sat in the bottom of a drawer for two years before I got the guts to try it again.

Something happened during that hibernation period. Maybe I matured as a knitter, or maybe I magically gained more patience. But mainly I just got tired of being intimidated. The next time I picked up that sock, the pattern clicked, and I

was instantly in love. That year I made a half-dozen pairs of socks, and I've never looked back. Everyone in my family has received socks as Christmas gifts, and I've replaced nearly all of my socks with hand-knit ones. I almost always have a sock-in-progress (or two) in my purse, just in case I have a few minutes of downtime during the day.

These days, socks are my favorite thing to knit. They're portable. They're (relatively) quick. And, with their infinite variations, they never get boring. Socks make amazing gifts, and simply put, they're the most fun to knit.

If you've never knit a pair of socks before- have no fear! Don't be like me and wait years before starting a sock only to banish it to the back of your closet. I'm here to show you that socks aren't nearly as scary (or as difficult) as they might seem. I guarantee, once you've finished your first sock, you'll become a sock addict, too!

- *Allison*

YARN & NEEDLES

I know your fingers are itching to start knitting, but we need to pause for a minute to do a little planning before you start working on your socks.

Let's talk yarn! We're knitters, after all, so that should be the fun part. Honestly, you can use almost any yarn to make socks, so really the sky's the limit. But you should keep a couple of guidelines in mind when you're picking out your yarn:

YARN

Weight
Thicker yarn creates thicker fabric. So, unless you're making slippers, stay away from bulky or worsted yarn (or your shoes might not fit!). I like using fingering-weight or sock-weight yarn for my everyday socks and slightly thicker sport-weight for my "lounging around the house watching TV on the weekends" socks.

Fiber content
A pair of socks takes a lot of abuse over the course of a day. Because of this, you'll want to use something springy yet tough. I love knitting with wool and wool blends when I make my socks. Wool is warm, light and springy, and any man-made fibers in the blend (like nylon or polyamide) add strength. If you don't do animal fibers, make sure that any blend you choose includes a little bit of spandex or Lycra for stretch (100% cotton socks get real droopy real quick).

Washability
I don't know about you, but I've got better things to do than hand-wash all my socks. Because of that, I always knit my socks with machine-washable yarn. I particularly love using superwash wool, it knits up like regular wool, but it's treated so that it doesn't felt when you throw your socks in the washing machine.

Examples In This Book
I've used Knit Picks' Stroll Sock Yarn (75% Superwash Merino Wool, 25% Nylon) to knit all the examples in this book. It's one of my favorites; soft, warm, and machine-washable. Plus, it comes in dozens of gorgeous colors! You'll need one 50g skein to make a pair of socks for a child, or two 50g skeins to make an adult pair.

NEEDLES
Once you've picked out your yarn, it's time to select your needles. Look at your yarn's label to see which size needles are suggested with your yarn. I love my US 2 (2.75mm)'s - they're not so tiny that I have trouble knitting, but they're small enough to make lovely smooth fabric, perfect for socks. Of course, US 2 (2.75mm)'s won't work for everyone. I am a bit of a tight knitter, but if you're a loose knitter you might want to go down a size or two. You should use whatever size feels right to you and your yarn. If you're using Knit Picks Stroll Sock Yarn, try needles in sizes US 1 (2.25mm), US 2 (2.75mm), or US 3 (3.25mm).

These instructions have been written using a set of five double-pointed needles (DPN's). I like using 5" or 6" long DPNs, because they fit comfortably in the palm of my hand. If you prefer longer or shorter needles, use those instead! Alternatively, you can knit socks using the Magic Loop or Two-Circulars techniques. It's all about what works best for you!

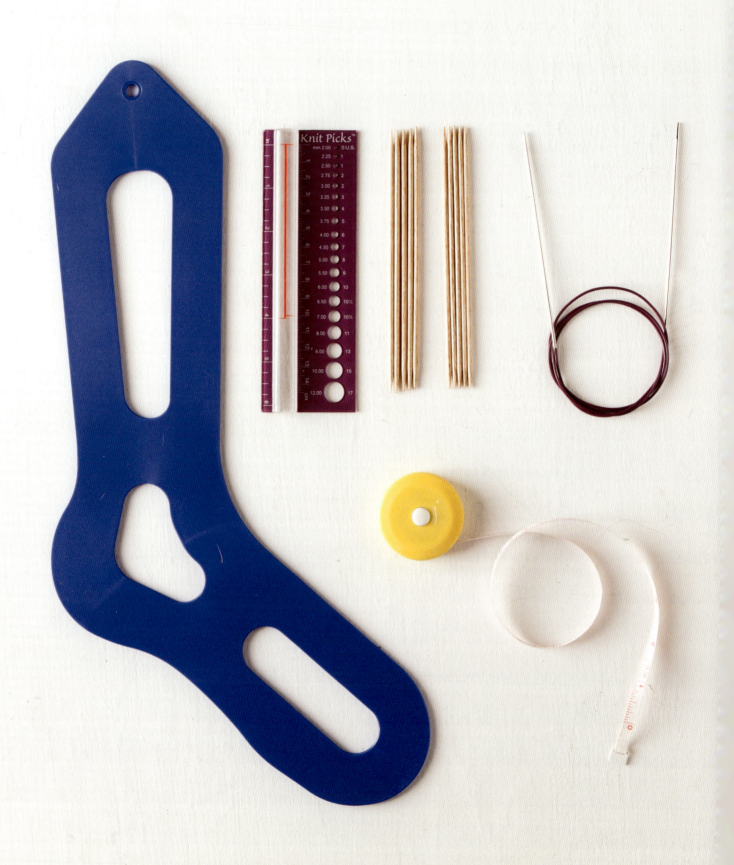

NOTIONS

One of my favorite aspects of sock knitting is its portability. A sock is a small project, knit on small needles, using just a few simple notions. Other than your yarn and needles, you probably already have everything you need.

SCISSORS
Of course you'll need a pair of scissors, what knitting project doesn't? I always keep a small pair in my sock-knitting bag.

YARN NEEDLE
You'll use this to weave in your ends. And depending on your design, you might need it for finishing a sewn bind off or a Kitchener Stitch toe.

TAPE MEASURE
(Optional, but recommended)
You'll need a tape measure to calculate your gauge and measure the size of your feet, believe it or not!

STITCH MARKERS
(Optional, but recommended)
While you don't technically need them, stitch markers are always a good idea to have on hand to help you remember when you get to the end of your round, or need to repeat a tricky design element. I like split-ring stitch markers for their versatility, but use whatever style you prefer.

NOTEBOOK
(Optional, but recommended)
No matter how hard I try not to be, I'm a forgetful person. By the time I start my second sock I have forgotten how I made the first one! So, I keep a little notebook in my sock bag, where I can keep my notes to make sure my socks will match.

KNITTING BAG
(Optional, but recommended)
I keep my socks-in-progress in a small zippered pouch along with my notes and all my notions. That way, I can throw them in my purse, backpack, or luggage, and I know my precious yarn will stay safe and untangled.

CROCHET HOOK
(Optional)
If you're doing any technique that requires a provisional cast on, you'll need a crochet hook. Find one that's a tiny bit bigger than your needles; it'll make your provisional cast on a lot easier. You might also use your crochet hook to fix any dropped stitches or other mistakes in your sock as you knit it up.

SCRAP YARN
(Optional)
If you're doing any technique that requires a provisional cast on, or if you plan on doing an afterthought heel (more on that later), you'll need smooth scrap yarn in a similar gauge as your sock yarn. Be sure to use scrap yarn that's a high-contrast color. You'll thank me later when you need to remove it!

CABLE NEEDLE
(Optional)
If you're making a cabled sock, you definitely need a cable needle. Use one that's close in size to your needles so you don't stretch out your stitches as you cable.

SOCK BLOCKERS
(Optional)
Sock blockers are an easy way to get professional-looking results when you block your socks. Make sure that you use a sock blocker that is the appropriate size for your socks—you don't want to stretch out your brand-new socks!

Little Waves Stitch Pattern, 1x1 Cuff, Afterthought Heel, & Standard Toe

GAUGE & SIZING

Calculating your gauge is the knitting-world equivalent of eating your vegetables. You know you should do it, but you never really want to. And most of the time (if we're being honest), that's OK. You can get away with a wonky gauge if you're making a blanket or a stuffed animal, but socks need to fit perfectly. No one wants a sock so big that it bunches up in your shoe or one that's so tight that it cuts off your circulation. When it comes to socks, I hate to say it, but you absolutely, positively must make a gauge swatch.

But don't worry, I'll walk you through the process and you'll see that it's not a big deal!

GAUGE

First, think about the sock you want to make; is it simple stockinette stitch, ribbed, or allover lace? I'm a fan of simple socks, so I'm making a swatch in stockinette stitch (knitting all rounds).

Once you've decided on your stitch pattern, it's time to start swatching. CO between 40 and 60 sts and work in the round for at least 3 or 4 inches. It's important to make a sock swatch in the round because you will also knit your sock in the round. Your gauge changes between working flat and in the round, even with the same needles and yarn. You should always make your swatch the same way you plan on making your project.

Once you've made your swatch, stretch it out slightly or if you're feeling really ambitious, block it. Then, use your tape measure to see how many sts are in 2" of your knitting. I have 14.5 sts in 2" of knitting. Divide that number by 2, to get your gauge (sts per inch). My gauge is 7.25 sts/inch. (Alternatively, you could measure the number of sts that fit into 1" of knitting, but if you do that, your measurement could end up a little less accurate.)

See, I told you that wouldn't be so bad!

Once you have determined your gauge, you can either put away your swatch or rip it out and reuse the yarn to make your sock.

SIZING

Now we know your gauge, but we still don't know how many stitches you're going to be working with. The missing information is... well... the size of your feet. For this step, you'll need a tape measure and a pair of bare feet from whomever will be receiving the socks.

Simply step on the tape measure and measure around the ball of your foot. You want this measurement to be nice and tight (but not so tight that it cuts off circulation). My foot circumference is about 9.5". Do this step carefully- it is important to be as accurate as possible. Make a note of your measurement in the table on page 61 for future reference.

If you're making these socks as a surprise for someone, or if you just can't find your tape measure, you can look at the Sock Size Chart on page 63 to find foot dimension estimates based on shoe size. But where's the fun in that?

Make sure to write down your gauge and foot circumference, you don't want to forget it!

Basket Weave Stitch Pattern, Reinforced Heel, & Standard Toe in Blue Topaz

TOP DOWN INSTRUCTIONS

Top down socks are worked, well, from the top to the toe. Because of their construction, they require little or no binding off, but do require casting on. Top down socks are great, classic socks, perfect for first-time sock knitters.

CUFF
Top down socks are begun at the cuff. Take a look at all of the cuff designs on page 29 and pick out the one that works best for your sock. You can use any stretchy cast on you prefer (unless otherwise stated), but if you use a long-tail cast on, be sure to cast on loosely. See Tutorials section for instructions on the Long Tail Cast On (pg 42), Provisional Cast On (pg 43) and Tubular Cast On (pg 44).

Ribbed Cuff
Ribbed cuffs are the old standby- they are structurally sound and stretchy, and they keep your socks in place even on a long day. A ribbed cuff can be as narrow as a few rows or as long as the entire leg of the sock.
Cast on (A)_____ sts. Distribute your sts evenly across 4 needles being careful not to twist, PM to mark the beginning of your round (optional) and join to work in the round. (You will have (C)_____ sts on each needle.) Choose either 1x1 or 2x2 rib and repeat the appropriate round until your cuff is the desired length.
1x1 Rib: (K1, P1) around.
2x2 Rib: (K2, P2) around.
Continue to the Leg section.

Rolled Cuff
Rolled cuffs are very simple to knit, and are a cute addition to feminine socks. However, they can get slouchy or droopy, and should be worked with a ribbed or otherwise structurally sound leg.
Cast on (A)_____ sts. Distribute your sts evenly across 4 needles being careful not to twist, PM to mark the beginning of your round (optional) and join to work in the round (You will have (C)_____ sts on each needle).
K around until sock measures 1" to 1.5". Allow the CO edge to naturally curl over and out.
Continue to the Leg section.

Faced Cuff
Faced cuffs lend a classic, old-fashioned style to socks. Both smooth and picot-edges give sock tops a lot of structure, although not a lot of elasticity
Cast on (A)_____ sts with provisional cast on leaving a very long tail (36+"). Distribute your sts evenly across 4 needles being careful not to twist, PM to mark the beginning of your round (optional) and join to work in the round (You will have (C)_____ sts on each needle). K until sock measures .5"-1". Then work the appropriate fold round

Fold Round Smooth Edge: P around.
Fold Round Picot Edge: (K2tog, YO) around.
K until sock measures .5"-1" from fold round (doubling sock length).
Continue to the Leg section.
Once you have completed your sock, follow the instructions in the Finishing section on page 27 to finish your faced cuff.

LEG
Once your cuff is done, it's time for the fun part- the leg! Think of it as a canvas where you get to stretch your legs (pardon the pun) and run wild with knitterly enthusiasm. Try stripes! Cables! Lace! Colorwork or textured patterns. Try an old favorite pattern, or something new. Try anything that strikes your fancy! The sky is the limit!
Or (if you're feeling minimalistic), you can skip this step entirely and go straight to the heel to make a short, ankle-length sock. It's up to you!

But, when deciding on your stitch pattern, keep two things in mind:
Gauge: Make sure your gauge remains constant. If you calculated gauge using a stockinette stitch swatch, but make a densely cabled sock, your gauge will be off, and your sock won't fit. For a proper fit, be sure to work your sock in the design you used to measure your gauge.
Stitch Count: You're good to go as long as your desired pattern fits into the number of sts on your needles. If you're concerned about doing math, any 2 or 4-stitch repeat will work well for socks.
Go ahead and experiment! Or, if you're not sure what to do, take a look at the Pattern Library on page 32 for some ideas. Once your leg reaches the desired length, continue to the Heel section.

HEEL
While it is possible to make a sock without a heel (that's what tube socks are, after all), hand-knit socks with perfectly-fitting heels are the best things you'll ever put on your feet. Of course, like everything with knitting, you've got tons of options, each with pros and cons. I've outlined how to work four classic heels that are sure to make your socks a real success. Take a look at the heel designs on page 30 to see all your options.
But before we begin working on your heel, let's check in with your needles. Be sure that your stitches are distributed evenly across all 4 needles ((C)_____ sts on each needle). Starting from the beginning of your round (where you placed your marker at the beginning of the cuff), number your needles clockwise from 1 to 4. Needles 1 and 4 will hold the

back of the heel and the sole of the foot, while Needles 2 and 3 will hold the top of the foot. Got it? Numbering your needles will really help to keep your stitches in order and your heel and toe pointing in the right direction.

On to the heels!

Note:
If you're working with Two Circulars or Magic Circle instead of using DPNs, instead of numbering your needles 1-4, think about dividing your stitches into quadrants or groups labeled 1 through 4. Start at the beginning of your round (the back of the heel), the next (C)_____ sts are Group 1, the next (C)_____ sts are Group 2, etc. Groups 1 and 4 will consist of stitches along the back of your heel and sole of your foot, while Groups 2 and 3 will include the stitches across the front of your leg and top of your foot.

Turned Heel

The turned heel is the quintessential sock heel. If you've ever wondered why hand-knit socks are so much more comfortable than store-bought ones, this is the reason. A sock with a properly turned heel actually has the shape of a human foot (which seems simple, but is surprisingly rare): wide at the ankle, then tapering down to the toe. Unfortunately, turning a heel can be a little intimidating the first couple times you do it- but don't fear! It's not as hard as it seems. You begin by using short rows to create a heel flap. Then you use wrap and turns (W&Ts) to create the round shape of the heel cap before decreasing sts on either side of the foot to make the gusset. Sure, a turned heel is a little tricky, but it's totally worth it. (See the page 52 of the Tutorials section for a refresher on these specialized techniques)

Directions

Begin by knitting across Needle 1. Turn your sock (you're knitting back and forth now).
Next Row (WS): SL 1, P across Needle 1. Then, using the same needle P across Needle 4. Set aside your spare needle. Turn. You've just combined Needles 1 and 4 onto a single needle. You will be working only these (B)_____ sts until you reach the gusset.

Heel Flap: Work the following 2 rows until you have worked (B)_____ heel flap rows, ending with Row 2.
Row 1 (RS): SL 1, K across needle, turn.
Row 2 (WS): SL 1, P across needle, turn.

Heel Cap: The heel cap is also worked back and forth, using W&Ts to shape. Find the W&T section on page 52 if you need a refresher.
Work the next 2 rows to set up the heel cap:
Row 1: K (C)_____ sts, place marker if you don't already have one in place, K2, K2tog, K1, W&T. 1 st dec.
Row 2: P to marker, SM, P2, SSP, P1, W&T. 1 st dec.
Repeat the following 2 rows until you are working across your whole needle, ending with Row 2. If you don't have room to complete an entire repeat, stop after the last complete Row 2 and continue to the Gusset section.
Row 1: K to 1 before the W&T gap (slipping the marker as you pass it), K2tog, K1, W&T. 1 st dec.
Row 2: P to 1 before the W&T gap (slipping the marker as you pass it), SSP, P1, W&T. 1 st dec.

Gusset: The gusset is worked in the round. Work set-up round as follows:
K to marker. Remove marker. With spare needle (that you set aside at the beginning of the heel), K to the end of the heel sts, then with the same needle, pick up (C)_____ sts along the left side of the heel flap. You have just knit across Needle 1. Work Needles 2 and 3 being sure to follow any patterns established while knitting the leg. With Needle 4, pick up (C)_____ sts on the right side of the heel flap, then knit the remaining heel sts.
Then, shape the gusset by repeating the following 2 rows until all of your needles hold (C)_____ sts, ending with Round 2.
Round 1: Needle 1: K to 2 before end, K2tog. Needle 2 and 3: Work in established pattern. Needle 4: SSK, K to end. 2 sts dec.
Round 2: Needle 1: K. Needle 2 and 3: Work in established pattern. Needle 4: K.
Continue to the Instep section.

Reinforced Heel

A reinforced heel is a variation on the classic turned heel. In a reinforced heel, the heel flap is worked in a slipped stitch pattern, creating thicker fabric where the heel rubs on the back of your shoe. A reinforced heel is perfect for people who are particularly hard on their socks (like me!).

Directions

Begin by knitting across Needle 1. Turn your sock (you're knitting back and forth now).
Next Row (WS): SL1, P across Needle 1. Then, using the same needle P across Needle 4. Set aside your spare needle. Turn. (You've just combined Needles 1 and 4 onto a single needle. You will be working only these (B)_____ sts until you reach the gusset.)

Heel Flap: Work the following 2 rows until you have worked (B)_____ heel flap rows, ending with Row 2.
Row 1 (RS): SL 1, K across needle, turn.
Row 2 (WS): (SL 1, P1) across needle, turn.
Then, follow the instructions for the turned heel, beginning at the heel cap.

Mitered Heel

A mitered heel is the kind of heel you see on store-bought socks. It's simple, classic and understated. However, a mitered heel doesn't provide quite as much room as a turned heel, so it's better for people with narrow feet or low arches. A mitered heel is worked using simple short-row shaping, and is a great way to practice your W&T technique (see the Tutorials section on page 52 for a refresher on how to work W&Ts).

Directions

Begin by working the following 2 set-up rows.
Row 1 (RS): K to 1 before the end of Needle 1. W&T. (You're knitting back and forth now).
Row 2 (WS): P across Needle 1. Then, use the same needle to P to 1 before the end of Needle 4. W&T. Set aside your spare needle. You've just combined Needles 1 and 4 onto a single needle. You will be working only these sts until you finish the heel.
Work the following two rows until 8-12 sts remain between the W&Ts, ending with Row 2. More sts between the W&Ts will lead to a shallower heel, fewer sts between the W&Ts will result in a pointier heel.
Row 1 (RS): K to 2 before W&T gap, W&T.
Row 2 (WS): P to 2 before W&T gap, W&T.
Then, work the bottom half of your heel by repeating the following two rows until you are again working across the entire heel. End with Row 2.
Row 1 (RS): SL1, K to 1 before next W&T gap, K1, knitting wrap with last st. Turn.
Row 2 (WS): SL1, P to 1 before next W&T gap, P1, purling wrap with last st. Turn.
Then, SL 1 and K halfway across your heel stitches ((C) _____ sts before the end of the needle). Pick up your spare needle, and work the following round:
Round 1: Needle 1: K, Needles 2 and 3: Work in established pattern, Needle 4: K.
Continue to the Instep section.

Afterthought Heel

An afterthought heel fits similarly to a mitered heel, but is worked completely differently (no short rows!). To create an afterthought heel, use scrap yarn to set aside stitches at the point where you want to insert a heel later. Then, once the rest of the sock is completed, those stitches are picked up and knit in the round with simple shaping to create the heel (hence the name). If short rows give you nightmares, the afterthought heel is the one for you!

Directions

Knit across Needle 1, work across Needles 2 and 3 in your established pattern. Then, set your working yarn aside, but do not break. With scrap yarn, K across Needles 4 and 1. Break scrap yarn. Pick up your working yarn, and K across Needle 4.

Note:
If you are working a striped sock, you might want to shift your afterthought heel (and your scrap yarn) to Needles 1 and 2, to avoid having to cut and weave in all those extra ends. If you choose to do this, remember to shift your toe one needle over as well, to keep your toe and heel lined up.

Continue to the Instep section. Once you have completed your sock, follow the instructions in the Finishing section on page 27 to finish your afterthought heel.

Instep

The instep is the part of the sock between the heel and the toe. Sometimes, the instep continues the pattern that you established for the leg; an all-over pattern looks quite elegant. Or, it's simple stockinette stitch, contrasting with a patterned leg. Of course, you can do anything you like, it's your sock after all! The only real rule is that the sole of the foot should be worked in stockinette stitch to give the wearer a smooth surface on which to walk.

Here's what you do:
Round 1: Needle 1: K, Needles 2 and 3: Work in desired pattern, Needle 4: K.
Repeat Round 1 until your sock measures 1" (for a child's sock), 1.5" (for a small adult's sock) or 2" (for a large adult's sock) *less than* the desired length, when measuring from back of heel to the needles.

Note:
If you are making a sock with an afterthought heel, measure your instep from the scrap yarn to your needles. Your instep will be finished when it is 2" (child's), 3" (small adult's) or 4" (large adult's) *less than* the desired foot length.

You can measure your desired foot length by standing on a tape measure and measuring from the back of the heel to the tip of the big toe. Or, you can use the Sock Size Chart (pg 63) to estimate your foot's length based on your shoe size.
Continue to the Toe section.

TOE

You're almost done! Hooray! All you have left to do is make your toe! And you've got choices here, too. There are two basic ways of working toes, standard and round. Both styles fit similarly, so your choice for your toe is mainly an aesthetic one. See page 30 for your options.

Standard Toe

A standard toe lays flat, with decreases lined up along each side of the foot for a smooth, classic shape.
Starting at the beginning of Needle 1 (the center of the sole), repeat the following 2 rows until 4-6 sts remain on each needle (16-24 total), ending with Round 2. More sts will lead to a shallower toe, fewer sts will result in a pointier toe.
Round 1: K.
Round 2: Needle 1: K to 2 before end, K2tog. Needle 2: SSK, K to end. Needle 3: K to 2 before end, K2tog. Needle 4: SSK, K to end. 4 sts dec.
Then, K to the end of Needle 1. Combine the sts from Needles 2 and 3 onto a single needle (top of foot). Combine the sts from Needles 1 and 4 onto a second needle (sole). Use the Kitchener Stitch to close up the toe (see Tutorial section pg 51 for instructions).
Continue to the Finishing section.

Round Toe

A round toe is worked by arranging decreases evenly around the toe for a smooth, organic shape.

Starting at the beginning of Needle 1 (the center of the sole), repeat the following 2 rows until 4-6 sts remain on each needle (16-24 total), ending with Round 2. More sts will lead to a shallower toe, fewer sts will result in a pointier toe.

Round 1: K.

Round 2: K around, evenly spacing 4 decreases across the round, staggering your decreases to avoid obvious decrease lines. Break the yarn, leaving an 18" tail. With a yarn needle, pull tail through active sts and pull tight.

Continue to the Finishing section.

Basket Weave Stitch Pattern, Reinforced Heel, & Standard Toe in Blue Topaz

Stockinette Stitch Pattern, Turned Heel, & Standard Toe in Dandelion

Broken Seed Stitch Pattern, Turned Heel, & Standard Toe in Pucker

TOE UP INSTRUCTIONS

Toe up socks are worked from the tip of the toe to the top of the cuff. Because of this, toe up socks do not use a traditional cast on, but do use a nice, stretchy bind off at the top of the leg. Toe up socks are a great way to get the most out of your yarn, because their construction lets you make the leg as long as possible before binding off, letting you use every last inch of yarn.

TOE

There are two basic ways of working toes, standard and round. Both styles fit similarly, so your choice for your toe is mainly an aesthetic one. See Tutorials section for Judy's Magic Cast On (pg 40), Provisional Cast On (pg 43), and Circular Cast On (pg 39).

Standard Toe

A standard toe lays flat, with decreases lined up along each side of the foot for a smooth, classic toe.

With Judy's Magic Cast On or a provisional cast on, CO 16, 20, or 24 sts, divided evenly over 2 needles and prepare to work in the round. More sts will lead to a shallower toe, fewer sts will result in a pointier toe.

Work the following two rounds twice.

Round 1: K.
Round 2: (K1, M1L, K to 1 st before end of needle, M1R, K1) twice. 4 sts inc.

Then, divide your sts evenly among 4 needles, and repeat the following two rounds until you have (A)_____ total sts ((C)_____ sts on each needle). Your increases should be lined up on either side of the toe.

Round 1: K.
Round 2: (K1, M1L, K to end of needle. K to 1 st before end of next needle, M1R, K1) twice. 4 sts inc.

End with Round 1, and continue to the Instep section.

Round Toe

A round toe is worked by arranging increases evenly around the toe for a smooth, organic toe shape.

With circle cast on or a provisional cast on, CO 16, 20, or 24 sts divided evenly over 4 needles. More sts will lead to a shallower toe, fewer sts will result in a pointier toe.

Work the following two rnds until you have (A)_____ total sts ((C)_____ sts on each needle).

Round 1: K.
Round 2: K, evenly spacing 4 increases across the round, staggering your increases to avoid obvious increase lines.
End with Round 1, and continue to the Instep section.

INSTEP

The instep is the part of the sock between the toe and the heel, and it's the first spot where you can really get creative with your pattern. Sometimes the pattern on the top of the instep will continue up the leg; an all-over pattern running from instep to leg looks quite elegant. Or, the instep can be simple stockinette stitch, contrasting with a patterned leg. If you want to have a pattern on the top of your foot, the time to start it is now. Of course, you can do anything you like, it's your sock after all! The only real rule is that the sole of the foot needs to be worked in stockinette stitch to give the wearer a smooth surface on which to walk.

The pattern you choose for your sock (whether you start working the pattern now, or once you hit the leg) is the fun part of making a sock. Think of your sock as a canvas, a project where you get to stretch your legs (pardon the pun) and run wild with knitterly enthusiasm. Try stripes! Cables! Lace! Even colorwork or textured patterns. Try an old favorite pattern, or something new. Try anything that strikes your fancy. The sky is the limit!

But, when deciding on your stitch pattern, keep two things in mind:

Gauge: Make sure your gauge remains constant. If you calculated gauge using a stockinette stitch swatch, then make a densely cabled sock, your gauge will be off, and your sock won't fit. For a proper fit, be sure to work your sock in the design you used to measure your gauge.

Stitch Count: You're good to go as long as your desired pattern fits into the number of sts on your needles. If you're concerned about doing math, any 2- or 4-st repeat will work well for socks.

Go ahead and experiment! Or, if you're not sure what to do, take a look at the Pattern Library on page 32 for some ideas.

Before you start working on your instep, let's check in with your needles. Be sure that your sts are distributed evenly across 4 needles ((C)_____ sts on each needle).

If you worked a standard toe, make sure that two of your needles lay along the top of the foot, and two lay along the bottom (the increases lay along the sides of the foot). Knit to the end of your next needle. This is now the beginning of your round, and the center of the bottom of your foot. Place marker, if desired.

If you worked a round toe, the orientation of your needles is less important (your toe is round, after all, so there isn't necessarily a "top" or "bottom"). Just make sure you've knit to the end of a needle. This is now the beginning of your round, and the center of the bottom of your foot. Place marker, if desired.

Starting from this point and moving clockwise, number your needles from 1 to 4. Needles 1 and 4 hold the sole of the foot and the back of the heel, while Needles 2 and 3 hold the top of the foot. Got it? It seems silly now, but numbering your needles will really help to keep your stitches in order and your heel and toe pointing in the right direction.

Note:
If you're working with Two Circulars or Magic Circle instead of using DPNs, instead of numbering your needles 1-4, think about dividing your stitches into quadrants or groups labeled 1 through 4. Start at the beginning of your round (the back of the heel), the next (C)_____ sts are Group 1, the next (C)_____ sts are Group 2, etc. Groups 1 and 4 will consist of stitches along the back of your heel and sole of your foot, while Groups 2 and 3 will include the stitches across the front of your leg and top of your foot.

Now that you've gotten your bearings, it's time to knit the instep. Here's what you do:
Round 1: Needle 1: K, Needles 2 and 3: Work in desired pattern, Needle 4: K.
If you plan on making a sock with a turned or reinforced heel, repeat Round 1 until your sock measures 1.5" (for a child's sock), 2.75" (for a small adult's sock) or 4" (for a large adult's sock) *less than* the desired length when measuring from the tip of the toe to the needles.

If you plan on making a sock with an afterthought or mitered heel, repeat Round 1 until your sock measures 1" (for a child's sock), 1.5" (for a small adult's sock) or 2" (for a large adult's sock) *less than* the desired length when measuring from the tip of the toe to the needles.

You can measure your foot length by standing on a tape measure and measuring from the back of the heel to the tip of the big toe. Or, you can use the Sock Table (pg 63) to estimate your foot's length based on your shoe size. Continue to the Heel section.

HEEL
While it is possible to make a sock without a heel (that's what tube socks are, after all), hand-knit socks with perfectly-fitting heels are the best things you'll ever put on your feet. Of course, like everything with knitting, you've got tons of options, each with pros and cons. I've outlined how to work four classic heels that are sure to make your socks a real success. Take a look at the heel designs on page 30 to see all your options.
On to the heels!

Turned Heel
The turned heel is the quintessential sock heel. If you've ever wondered why hand-knit socks are so much more comfortable than store-bought ones, this is the reason. A sock with a properly turned heel actually has the shape of a human foot (which seems simple, but is surprisingly rare): wide at the ankle, then tapering down to the toe. Unfortunately, turning a heel can be a little intimidating the first couple times you do it- but don't fear! It's not as hard as it seems. Begin by increasing stitches at either side of the foot to form the gusset. Then use wrap and turns (W&Ts) to create the round shape of the heel cap, before using short rows and decreasing your way up the heel flap. Sure, the turned heel is a little tricky, but it's totally worth it. (See page 52 of the Tutorials section for a refresher on how to work W&Ts.)

Directions
Gusset: Work the following 2 rounds until you have (D)_____ sts on your needles, ending with Row 2. (Look at the Stitch Count Chart on page 63 to find your value for (D).)
Round 1: Needle 1: K to 1 st before end, M1R, K1. Needles 2 and 3: Work in pattern. Needle 4: K1, M1L, K to end. 2 sts inc.
Round 2: Needle 1: K, Needles 2 and 3: Work in pattern, Needle 4: K.

Heel Cap: Work the following 2 rows to set up heel cap.
Note: The heel is worked back and forth using short rows from now on. (See the Tutorials section on page 52 for a refresher on W&T. See the Stitch Count Chart on page 63 to find your value for (E).)
Row 1 (RS): Needle 1: K (E)_____ sts, KFB, K1, W&T. 1 st inc.
Row 2 (WS): Needle 1: P to end. Needle 4: P (E)_____ sts, PFB, P1, W&T. 1 st inc.
Then, work the following 2 rows until you can no longer fit another full repeat between your W&Ts, ending with Row 2.
Row 1 (RS): Needle 4: K to end. Needle 1: K to 6 sts before W&T gap, KFB, K1, W&T. 1 st inc.
Row 2 (WS): Needle 1: P to end. Needle 4: P to 6 sts before W&T gap, PFB, P1, W&T. 1 st inc.

Heel Flap: Work the following 2 rows to set up the heel flap, continuing to work back and forth.
Row 1 (RS): Needle 4: K to end. Needle 1: K to 1 before furthest W&T gap, working wraps as you go, SSK, turn. 1 st dec.
Row 2 (WS): Needle 1: SL 1, P to end. Needle 4: P to 1 before furthest W&T gap, working wraps as you go, P2tog, turn. 1 st dec.
Then repeat the following 2 rows until only (A)_____ sts remain total ((C)_____ sts on each needle), ending with Row 2.
Row 1 (RS): Needle 4: SL 1, K to end. Needle 1: K to 1 before gap, SSK, turn. 1 st dec.
Row 2 (WS): Needle 1: SL 1, P to end. Needle 4: P to 1 before gap, P2tog, turn. 1 st dec.
Then, SL 1 and K across Needle 4.
Continue to the Leg section.

Reinforced Heel

A reinforced heel is a variation on the classic turned heel. In a reinforced heel, the heel flap is worked in a slipped stitch pattern, creating thicker fabric where the heel rubs on the back of your shoe. A reinforced heel is perfect for people who are particularly hard on their socks (like me!).

Directions

Gusset: Work the following 2 rounds until you have (D)_____ sts on your needles, ending with Row 2. (Look at the Stitch Count Chart on page 63 to find your value for (D).)
Round 1: Needle 1: K to 1 st before end, M1R, K1. Needles 2 and 3: Work in pattern. Needle 4: K1, M1L, K to end. 2 sts inc.
Round 2: Needle 1: K, Needles 2 and 3: Work in pattern, Needle 4: K.

Heel Cap: Work the following 2 rows to set up heel cap.
Note: The heel is worked back and forth using short rows from now on. (See the Tutorials section on page 52 for a refresher on W&T. See the Stitch Count Chart on page 63 to find your value for (E).)
Row 1 (RS): Needle 1: K (E)_____ sts, KFB, K1, W&T. 1 st inc.
Row 2 (WS): Needle 1: P to end. Needle 4: P (E)_____ sts, PFB, P1, W&T. 1 st inc.
Then, work the following 2 rows until you can no longer fit another full repeat between your W&Ts, ending with Row 2.
Row 1 (RS): Needle 4: K to end. Needle 1: K to 6 sts before W&T gap, KFB, K1, W&T. 1 st inc.
Row 2 (WS): Needle 1: P to end. Needle 4: P to 6 sts before W&T gap, PFB, P1, W&T. 1 st inc.

Heel Flap: Work the following 2 rows to set up the heel flap, continuing to work back and forth:
Row 1 (RS): Needle 4: K to end. Needle 1: K to 1 before furthest W&T gap, working wraps as you go, SSK, turn. 1 st dec.
Row 2 (WS): Needle 1: SL 1, P to end. Needle 4: P to 1 before furthest W&T gap, working wraps as you go, P2tog, turn. 1 st dec.
Then repeat the following 2 rows until only (A)_____ sts remain total ((C)_____ sts on each needle), ending with Row 2.
Row 1 (RS): Needle 4: SL 1, K to end. Needle 1: K to 1 before gap, SSK, turn. 1 st dec.
Row 2 (WS): Needles 1 and 4: (SL 1, P1) across both needles to 1 before gap, P2tog, turn. 1 st dec.
Then, SL 1 and K across Needle 4.
Continue to the Leg section.

Mitered Heel

A mitered heel is the kind of heel you see on store-bought socks. It's simple, classic and understated. However, a mitered heel doesn't provide quite as much room as a turned heel, so it's better for people with narrow feet or low arches. A mitered heel is worked using simple short-row shaping, and is a great way to practice your W&T technique (see page 52 the Tutorials section for a refresher on how to work W&Ts).

Directions

Begin by working the following 2 set-up rows.
Row 1 (RS): K to 1 before the end of Needle 1. W&T. (You're knitting back and forth now).
Row 2 (WS): P across Needle 1. Then, use the same needle to P to 1 before the end of Needle 4. W&T. Set aside your spare needle. You've just combined Needles 1 and 4 onto a single needle. You will be working only these sts until you finish the heel.
Work the following two rows until 8-12 sts remain between the W&Ts, ending with Row 2. More sts between the W&Ts will lead to a shallower heel, fewer sts between the W&Ts will result in a pointier heel.
Row 1 (RS): K to 2 before W&T gap, W&T.
Row 2 (WS): P to 2 before W&T gap, W&T.
Then, work the bottom half of your heel by repeating the following two rows until you are again working across the entire heel. End with Row 2.
Row 1 (RS): SL1, K to 1 before next W&T gap, K1, knitting wrap with last st. Turn.
Row 2 (WS): SL1, P to 1 before next W&T gap, P1, purling wrap with last st. Turn.
Then, SL 1 and K halfway across your heel stitches ((C)_____ sts before the end of the needle). Pick up your spare needle, and work the following round:
Round 1: Needle 1: K, Needles 2 and 3: Work in established pattern, Needle 4: K.
Continue to the Leg section.

Afterthought Heel

An afterthought heel fits similarly to a mitered heel, but is worked completely differently (no short rows!). To create an afterthought heel, use scrap yarn to set aside stitches at the point where you want to insert a heel later. Then, once the rest of the sock is completed, those stitches are picked up and knit in the round with simple shaping to create the heel (hence the name). If short rows give you nightmares, the afterthought heel is the one for you!

Directions

Knit across Needle 1, work across Needles 2 and 3 in your established pattern. Then, set your working yarn aside, but do not break. With scrap yarn, K across Needles 4 and 1. Break scrap yarn. Pick up your working yarn, and K across Needle 4.

Note: If you are working a striped sock, you might want to shift your afterthought heel (and your scrap yarn) to Needles 1 and 2, to avoid having to cut and weave in all those extra ends. If you choose to do this, remember to make sure your toe and heel are lined up.

Continue to the Leg section. Once you have completed your sock, follow the instructions in the Finishing section on page 27 to finish your afterthought heel.

LEG

Once your heel is done, it's time for the fun part- the leg! Without any shaping, this is the simplest part of the sock. If you haven't already established a fancy pattern for your sock, now is the time to do it. (Or don't! It's your sock!) Work in the round without any shaping until your sock is almost as long as desired (remember, you're going to do a cuff on top).
Or, if you're feeling minimalistic, you can skip this step entirely and go straight to the cuff to make a short sock. It's up to you!

CUFF

The last part of the sock is the cuff. Take a look at all of the cuff designs on page 29, and pick out the one that works best for your design. You can use any stretchy bind off you prefer (unless otherwise stated), but if you use a standard bind off (see page 50 of the Tutorials section), be sure to work it loosely. Jeny's Surprisingly Stretchy Bind Off (pg 47) and the sewn bind off (pg 49) are great alternatives.

Ribbed Cuff

Ribbed cuffs are the old standby. They are structurally sound and stretchy, and keep your socks in place even on a long day. A ribbed cuff can be as narrow as a few rows or as long as the entire leg of the sock.
Choose either 1x1 or 2x2 rib, and repeat the appropriate round until your cuff is the desired length.
For 1x1 Rib: (K1, P1) around.
For 2x2 Rib: (K2, P2) around.
Bind off very loosely, or use a stretchy bind off.

Rolled Cuff

Rolled cuffs are very simple to knit, and are a cute addition to feminine socks. However, they tend to get slouchy or droopy, and should be worked with a ribbed or otherwise structurally sound leg.

K around until cuff measures 1" to 1.5", allowing the fabric to naturally curl over and out.
BO very loosely, or use a stretchy bind off.

Faced Cuff

Faced cuffs lend a classic, old-fashioned style to socks. Both smooth and picot-edges give sock tops a lot of structure, though not a lot of elasticity.

K around until cuff measures .5"-1". Then work the appropriate fold round.
Fold Round Smooth Edge: P 1 row.
Fold Round Picot Edge: (K2tog, YO) around.
K until sock measures .5"-1" from fold round (doubling cuff length).
Break yarn, leaving a very long (36"+) tail.
Turn your sock inside-out. (Faced Cuff Figure 1, pg 56) Fold the cuff toward the inside of the sock along the fold round (Faced Cuff Figure 2, pg 56). Use the long tail and a yarn needle to sew each active st to a purl bump directly below it, being sure to keep your sts slightly loose and invisible from the outside. (Faced Cuff Figure 3 and 4, pg 57)

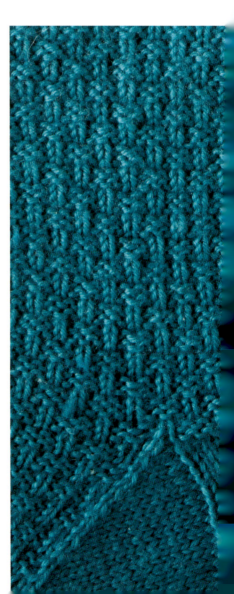

One Row Stripes Stitch Pattern, Standard Toe, & Afterthought Heel in Black, White, & Pucker

Stockinette Stitch Pattern, Turned Heel, & Standard Toe in Dandelion

FINISHING

Congratulations! You've made a sock! (Almost.) If you've chosen to make an afterthought heel, or used a technique that uses a provisional CO, use the following instructions to complete those features. Otherwise, skip ahead to finish up your sock!

AFTERTHOUGHT HEEL

(see the photo tutorial on pg 57 for assistance in starting the heel).

Make your heel: Carefully remove your scrap yarn, picking up the live sts as you go. Feel free to carefully cut your scrap yarn to help free your heel sts, just don't cut your sock! You will end up with your sts arranged on two needles; one on the leg edge (top), and one on the foot edge (bottom). Divide your sts evenly onto 4 needles, being sure you have (C)_____ sts on each needle. Number your needles from 1 to 4, starting at the center of the sole and moving clockwise (Afterthought Heel Figure 4, pg 58). Join your yarn at the beginning of Needle 1 and prepare to work in the round. Repeat the following 2 rows until 4-6 sts remain on each needle (16-24 total), ending with Round 2. More sts will lead to a shallower heel, fewer sts will result in a pointier heel.

Round 1: K.

Round 2: Needle 1: K to 2 before end, K2tog. Needle 2: SSK, K to end. Needle 3: K to 2 before end, K2tog. Needle 4: SSK, K to end. 4 sts dec.

Then, K to the end of Needle 1. Combine the sts from Needles 2 and 3 onto a single needle (top of heel). Combine the sts from Needles 1 and 4 onto a second needle (bottom of heel). Use the Kitchener Stitch to close up the heel (see page 51 of the Tutorial section for instructions).

TOP DOWN FACED CUFF

(see the photo tutorial on pg 56).

Turn your sock inside-out and remove the provisional CO, transferring all (A)_____ sts to your needles. Fold the cuff toward the inside of the sock along the fold round. Use the long tail and a yarn needle to sew each active st to a purl bump directly below it, being sure to keep your sts slightly loose and invisible from the outside.

TOE UP STANDARD TOE (PROVISIONAL CAST ON)

Carefully remove the provisional cast on (see "Removing Provisional Cast On" tutorial on pg 44), picking up the live sts and arranging them on two needles (one on the top of the foot and one on the bottom). Use the Kitchener Stitch to close up the toe (see page 51 of the Tutorial section for detailed instructions).

TOE UP ROUND TOE (PROVISIONAL CAST ON)

Carefully remove the provisional cast on (see "Removing Provisional Cast On" tutorial on pg 44), picking up the live sts and arranging them on several needles. Use a yarn needle to pull the tail yarn through the active sts and pull tight.

ALL METHODS

Now, all that's left to do is weave in your tails, trimming the ends to about 1" and letting them dangle on the inside of your sock. Your sock is ready to wear!

BLOCKING (OPTIONAL)

But, if you've got the time, consider blocking your socks. Blocking is magical. It's like ironing a nice dress- the dress might look fine before it's ironed, but it will look amazing after. I like to wet-block my socks. I soak them in warm water for 10-20 minutes (or until I remember I left them in the sink). Then I carefully wring them out by rolling them in a towel-don't pull, scrunch, or agitate your wet knitting- that way lies felted socks! Then, I lay them flat on a dry towel, smoothing out any bumps or weird shapes. Or, if you have them, you can slip your wet socks onto sock blockers and hang them to dry. Either way, once your socks have dried, you are ready to go!

(Now you just have to make the second one...)

Openwork Stripes Stitch Pattern & Standard Toe in Electric Blue

CUFF, TOE, & HEEL LIBRARY

CUFFS

1x1 Ribbing

2x2 Ribbing

Rolled Cuff

Faced Cuff - Smooth Edge

Faced Cuff - Picot Edge

TOES

Standard Toe

Round Toe

HEELS

Turned Heel

Reinforced Heel

Mitered Heel

Afterthought Heel

One Row Stripes Stitch Pattern & Afterthought Heel in Black, White, & Pucker

PATTERN LIBRARY

Socks are a great way to try new techniques and stitches without committing to a giant sweater or afghan. You're free to use any texture, pattern, stripe or design on your socks, but I've written out a handful of patterns that I love using for my socks. These patterns are written to be worked in the round over a multiple of 4 sts unless otherwise stated. Rounds should be repeated as desired, depending on the design and length of your sock. All socks shown in Knit Picks Stroll (75% Superwash Merino Wool, 25% Nylon, 231 yds/50g).

SIMPLE

You can't get any simpler than Stockinette stitch and Reverse Stockinette stitch! But simple isn't a bad thing. Socks worked in these patterns are classics, sure to be worn every day.

Stockinette Stitch
All Rounds: K around.

Shown in
Dandelion 25024

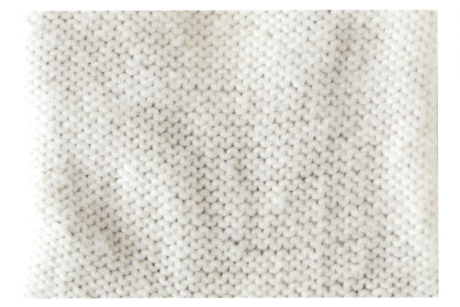

Reverse Stockinette Stitch
All Rounds: P around.

Shown in
White 26082

STRIPES

Stripes are perfect for socks, because they add fun detail to even the simplest socks. And, if you make your stripes thin enough you can work them without breaking your yarn (no extra ends to weave in!). At the end of each round, simply drop the yarn that you are not using, and pick up the one that you want to use next. Just be sure to avoid pulling the un-used yarn too tightly, or you can end up with unsightly (and uncomfortable) pulls in your sock. Try different color combinations and see how they turn out!

1-Row Stripes

Round 1: K around with MC.
Round 2: K around with C1.
Repeat Rounds 1-2

Shown in
Black 23701
White 26082

Oddball Stripes

Experiment by varying the number of rounds of each color to make different stripe patterns, or even random stripes.

Shown in
Electric Blue 26406
White 26082

CABLES

Cabled fabric's gauge varies greatly from Stockinette stitch, so be sure to check your gauge before making a cabled sock. If you're worried about your cabled fabric being too thick, try working one or two cables up the sides of the leg, instead of many cables all the way around.

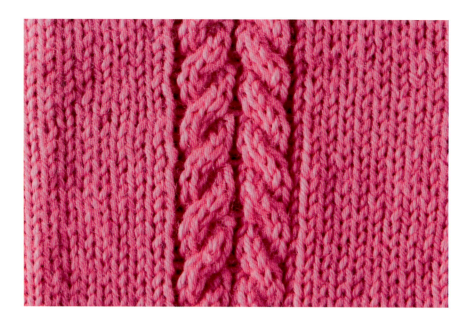

Twin Cable
(worked over any number of sts)

Round 1: Needle 1: K to 5 before end, P1, SL2 to CN, hold behind, K2, K2 from CN, Needle 2: P1, SL2 to CN, hold in front, K2, K2 from CN, P1, K to end, Needle 3: K to 6 before end, P1, SL2 to CN, hold behind, K2, K2 from CN, P1, Needle 4: SL2 to CN, hold in front, K2, K2 from CN, P1, K to end.
Rounds 2-4: Needle 1: K to 5 before end, P1, K4, Needle 2: P1, K4, P1, K to end, Needle 3: K to 6 before end, P1, K4, P1, Needle 4: K4, P1, K to end.
Repeat Rounds 1-4.

Shown in
Pucker 26401

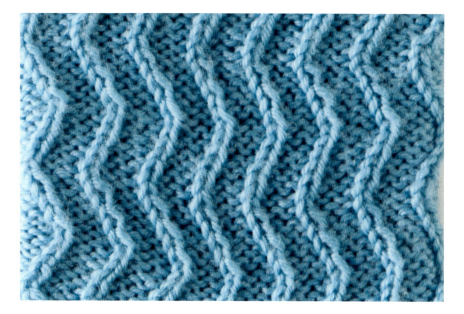

Little Waves

Round 1: (SL1 to CN and hold in front, P1 from LH needle, K1 from CN, P2) around.
Round 2: (P1, K1, P2) around.
Round 3: (P1, SL1 to CN and hold in front, P1 from LH needle, K1 from CN, P1) around.
Round 4: (P2, K1, P1) around.
Round 5: (P2, SL1 to CN and hold in front, P1 from LH needle, K1 from CN) around.
Round 6: (P3, K1) around.
Round 7: (P2, SL1 to CN and hold in back, K1 from LH needle, P1 from CN) around.
Round 8: (P2, K1, P1) around.
Round 9: (P1, SL1 to CN and hold in back, K1 from LH needle, P1 from CN, P1) around.
Round 10: (P1, K1, P2) around.
Round 11: (SL1 to CN and hold in back, K1 from LH needle, P1 from CN, P2) around.
Round 12: (K1, P3) around.
Repeat Rounds 1-12.

Shown in
Electric Blue 26406

KNIT/PURL TEXTURES

Some of my favorite socks feature simple knit/purl textures. They are nice and sturdy, dead simple to work up, and totally unisex. Perfect for everyday socks, knit/purl textures are a great way for even the most beginner sock knitter to make something beautiful.

Broken Seed Stitch
(worked over an even number of sts)

Round 1: K around.
Round 2: (K1, P1) around.
Round 3: K around.
Round 4: (P1, K1) around.
Repeat Rounds 1-4.

Shown in Pucker 26401

Basket Weave

Round 1: K around.
Rounds 2-3: (P3, K1) around.
Round 4: K around.
Rounds 5-6: (P1, K1, P2) around.
Repeat Rounds 1-6.

Shown in Blue Topaz 25019

KNIT/PURL TEXTURES (cont.)

Swirl

Round 1: K around.
Round 2: (K3, P1) around.
Round 3: K around.
Round 4: (K2, P1, K1) around.
Round 5: K around.
Round 6: (K1, P1, K2) around.
Round 7: K around.
Round 8: (P1, K3) around.
Repeat Rounds 1–8.

Shown in
Blue Topaz 25019

Swirl Stitch Pattern, Round Toe, & Turned Heel in Blue Topaz

OPENWORK

Openwork designs are beautiful, and make for lovely, feminine socks. Just be aware that socks with too much openwork have a tendency to wear out faster than those with more substantial stitch work.

Tiny Dots

Rounds 1-2: K around.
Round 3: (K2, SSK, YO) around.
Rounds 4-5: K around
Round 6: (SSK, YO, K2) around.
Repeat Rounds 1-6.

Shown in
White 26082

Openwork Stripes

Round 1-5: K around.
Round 6: (K1, K2tog, YO, K1) around.
Round 7: (K2tog, YO) around.
Round 8: (K1, K2tog, YO, K1) around.
Repeat Rounds 1-8.

Shown in
Electric Blue 26406

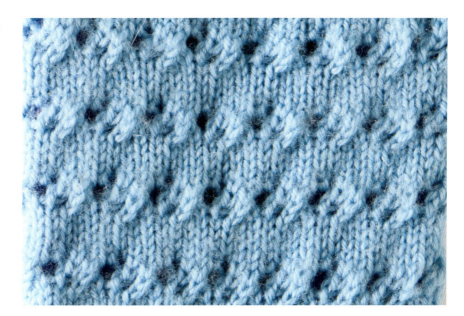

TUTORIALS

Socks require a handful of fairly specialized techniques to get the best results. Sometimes these techniques can be a little overwhelming or intimidating. In this section, I've included tutorials to get you through the toughest parts of sock making. For more help, see Knit Picks' "Go Your Own Way Socks" video tutorials on the Knit Picks website. The "Toe Up" version can be found here: http://tutorials.knitpicks.com/category/go-your-own-way-socks-toe-up/ and the "Top Down" version can be found here: http://tutorials.knitpicks.com/category/go-your-own-way-socks-top-down/.

CAST ONS

These cast on techniques are all pretty specialized, so be sure to look at your pattern to determine which technique is the best for your sock. Top down socks can begin with a long-tail cast on (simple, but not terribly stretchy), or a tubular cast on (more complicated, but very stretchy). Toe up socks use Judy's Magic Cast On (for standard toes) or the circular cast on (for round toes). The provisional cast on is a very versatile cast on that can be used for toe up socks and for top down socks with a faced cuff.

CIRCULAR CAST ON

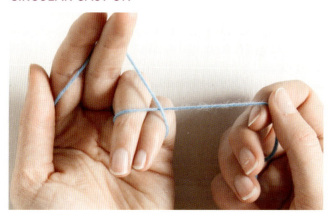

Circular Cast On, Fig.1

Begin by wrapping your yarn in a loop around your left ring and pinky fingers, holding your working yarn in with your left index and middle fingers. Your tail yarn will fall underneath the working yarn. Be sure to leave a long (18") tail.

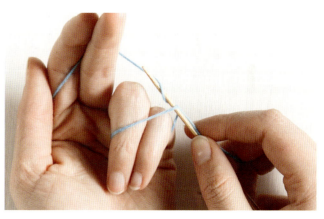

Circular Cast On, Fig.2

Step 1: Insert your needle into the loop, then up and over the working yarn, pulling the working yarn through the loop and creating a stitch (Circular Cast On Figures 2 and 3).

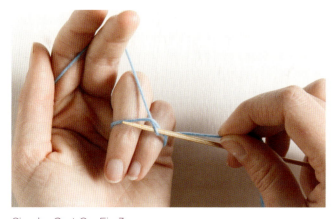

Circular Cast On, Fig.3

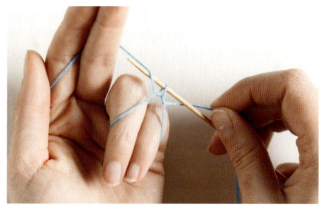

Circular Cast On, Fig.4

Step 2: Make the next stitch by wrapping the working yarn around the needle from front to back (like a yarn over).

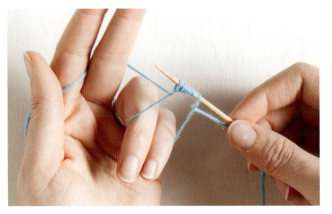

Circular Cast On, Fig.5

Repeat Steps 1 and 2 until you have the desired number of stitches on your needle, ending with Step 2 for an even number.

Circular Cast On, Fig.6

Tug on the tail to tighten the loop, if it gets too big.

Circular Cast On, Fig.7

Divide your stitches among the desired number of needles and prepare to work in the round.

JUDY'S MAGIC CAST ON

Begin by making a slipknot, leaving a long (18") tail. Hold 2 needles in your right hand, and place the slipknot onto the top needle (Needle 1).

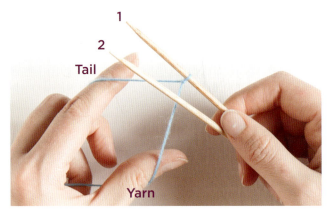

Judy's Magic Cast On, Fig.1

Then, wrap the tail around your right index finger, and your working yarn around your left thumb.

Judy's Magic Cast On, Fig.2

Step 1: Wrap the tail (index finger) around Needle 2 from the outside in.

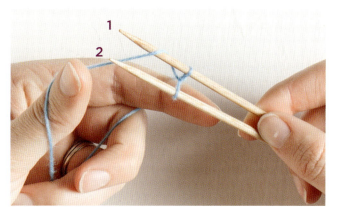

Judy's Magic Cast On, Fig.3
Step 2: Wrap the working yarn (thumb) around Needle 1 from the outside in.

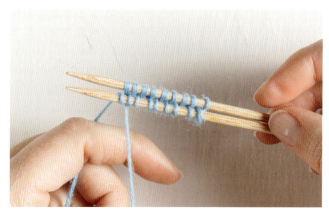

Judy's Magic Cast On, Fig.4
Repeat Steps 1 and 2 until you have the total desired stitches cast on (ending with Step 1 for an even number of stitches). Be sure to count the stitches on both needles.

Judy's Magic Cast On, Fig.5
Knit across Needle 1, using a third needle.

Judy's Magic Cast On, Fig.6
Turn, and knit across Needle 2.

Judy's Magic Cast On, Fig.7
Continue on to chosen toe.

LONG-TAIL CAST ON

Begin by making a slip knot, leaving a very long (40+") tail. Hold a needle in your right hand and slip the knot onto it, making it snug. (Long-Tail Cast On Figure 1.)

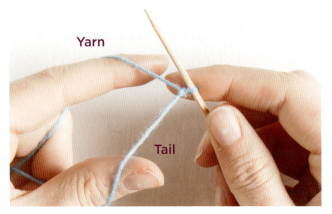

Long-Tail Cast On, Fig.1

Step 1: Wrap the working yarn around your left index finger, and the tail around your left thumb as shown. Hold both strands against your palm with your ring and pinky fingers.

Long-Tail Cast On, Fig.2

Step 2: Run the tip of the needle from the base of your thumb, up, passing through the thumb loop.

Long-Tail Cast On, Fig.3

Step 3: Run the tip of your needle from the tip of your index finger down, catching the index finger loop.

Long-Tail Cast On, Fig.4

Step 4: Then, run the tip of the needle from the tip of your thumb, down, reversing the direction of Step 1, going back out of the thumb loop.

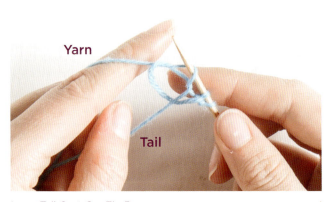

Long-Tail Cast On, Fig.5

Step 5: Remove your thumb from its loop, and snug up the yarn until a stitch is formed around the needle (Long-Tail Cast On Figure 5 and 6).

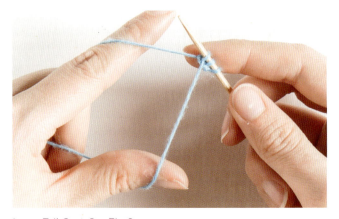

Long-Tail Cast On, Fig.6

Long-Tail Cast On, Fig.7

Repeat Steps 1-5 until you have the desired number of stitches on your needle (the slip knot at the beginning of the cast on counts as one stitch).

PROVISIONAL CAST ON

Begin with scrap yarn of a similar weight to the working yarn, but in a contrasting color. Using a crochet hook of similar size to your needles, loosely crochet a chain of about 10 more stitches than desired for cast on. Then, with your working yarn, complete the following steps:

Provisional Cast On Set Up

Provisional Cast On, Fig.1

Step 1: Turn the chain over, exposing the bumps on the back. Slide your needle into a bump near the beginning of the chain.

Provisional Cast On, Fig.2

Step 2: Wrap your yarn around the needle, as if knitting a normal stitch.
Step 3: Pull yarn through chain bump, creating a stitch.

Provisional Cast On, Fig.3

Step 4: Repeat steps 1-3, working your way along the crochet chain, until you have cast on your total number of desired stitches (Provisional Cast On Figures 3-4).

Provisional Cast On, Fig.4

Tutorials 43

Removing the Provisional Cast On

Provisional Cast On, Fig.5
Once your piece is completed, you will need to remove the scrap yarn.

Provisional Cast On, Fig.6
Step 1: Carefully snip the scrap yarn every few stitches, being sure not to cut your sock yarn.

Provisional Cast On, Fig.7
Step 2: Gently remove the scrap yarn, exposing live stitches a few at a time. Pick up the live stitches with your needle.

Provisional Cast On, Fig.8
Step 3: Continue until scrap yarn has been removed and all the live stitches have been picked up. Then, continue with your pattern as written.

TUBULAR CAST ON

This cast on is particularly well-suited for 1x1 rib cuffs, but its neat and stretchy appearance will allow it to work well for any top-down cuff. The tubular cast on is worked flat.

Tubular Cast On, Fig.1
Step 1: With scrap yarn, use your favorite cast on to CO half your desired number of stitches. Break yarn.

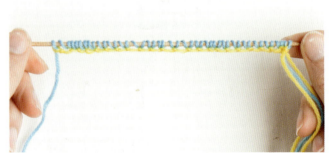

Tubular Cast On, Fig.2
Step 2: Change to working yarn. (K1, YO) to 1 before end. K1. Turn.

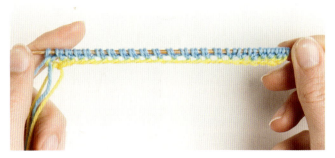

Tubular Cast On, Fig.3

Step 3: Work next row: (Bring yarn forward, SL1, bring yarn back, K1) to 1 before end. Bring yarn forward, SL1. (*Note:* You've just knit into your YOs from Step 2). Turn.

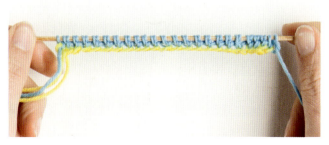

Tubular Cast On, Fig.4

Step 4: Work next row: (K1, bring yarn forward, SL1, bring yarn back) to 1 before end. K1. Turn.

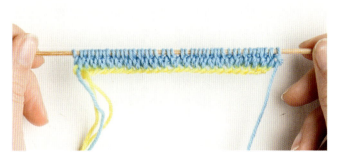

Tubular Cast On, Fig.5

Step 5: Repeat Steps 3 and 4 once more.

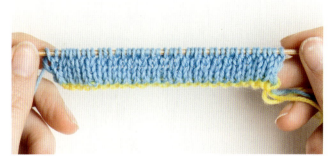

Tubular Cast On, Fig.6

Step 6: Work one row of 1x1 rib, beginning with a P. If working in the round as for socks, divide your stitches evenly among 4 needles, and work in established pattern in the round for at least 1 round before changing stitch pattern for Cuff. Once you have worked a few more rounds, continue to Step 7.

Tubular Cast On, Fig.7

Step 7: Remove the scrap yarn, carefully snipping it away from your cast on edge (Figues 7-8).

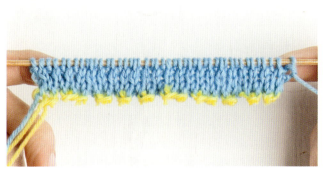

Tubular Cast On, Fig.8

Tutorials 45

Tubular Cast On, Fig.9
Step 8: Gently pull scrap yarn out of stitches.

Tubular Cast On, Fig.10
Your cast on is complete!

Reverse Stockinette Stitch Pattern, Standard Toe, & Afterthought Heel in White

BIND OFFS

These bind offs can be used for finishing the tops of toe-up socks. The standard bind off is simplest and looks very neat, but must be worked very loosely to avoid a too-tight sock top. Jeny's Surprisingly Stretchy Bind Off and the sewn bind off are both very stretchy, but are a little more involved. Use the bind off that feels right for you.

JENY'S SURPRISINGLY STRETCHY BIND OFF

This bind off is perfect for ribbed cuffs, but you'll need to pay attention to what you are doing because knit and purl stitches are worked slightly differently. This tutorial is shown with a 2x2 cuff. If working a cuff with a different ribbing pattern, alternate between the "Working Knit Stitches" and "Working Purl Stitches" sections as the pattern dictates.

Working Knit Stitches

Jeny's Surprisingly Stretchy Bind Off, Fig.1
Step 1: Yarn Over (YO) purl-wise (back to front).

Jeny's Surprisingly Stretchy Bind Off, Fig.2
Step 2: Knit 1.

Jeny's Surprisingly Stretchy Bind Off, Fig.3
Step 3: Pass YO over knit stitch and off the needle.

Jeny's Surprisingly Stretchy Bind Off, Fig.4
Step 4: Repeat steps 1-3 for second knit stitch.

Jeny's Surprisingly Stretchy Bind Off, Fig.5

Step 5: Pass right stitch over left stitch and off the needle (Figures 5-6).

Jeny's Surprisingly Stretchy Bind Off, Fig.6

Working Purl Stitches

Jeny's Surprisingly Stretchy Bind Off, Fig.7

Step 6: YO Knit-wise (front to back).

Jeny's Surprisingly Stretchy Bind Off, Fig.8

Step 7: Purl 1.

Jeny's Surprisingly Stretchy Bind Off, Fig.9

Step 8: Pass YO over purl stitch and off the needle.

Jeny's Surprisingly Stretchy Bind Off, Fig.10

Step 9: Pass remaining right stitch over left stitch and off the needle.

Jeny's Surprisingly Stretchy Bind Off, Fig.11

Step 10: Repeat steps 6-9 for second purl stitch, then continue working knit and purl stitches until all but 1 stitch has been bound off. Break yarn, leaving a long tail. Pass tail through the active stitch.

SEWN BIND OFF

Break your yarn, leaving a very long (40+") tail. Thread tail through a yarn needle. Be sure to pull your yarn snug, but not tight, after each step.

Sewn Bind Off, Fig.1

Step 1: Insert your yarn needle from right to left through the first 2 stitches and pull yarn tail through. Do not drop stiches off the needle

Sewn Bind Off, Fig.2

Step 2: Insert your yarn needle from left to right through the first stitch (that you've already sewn through).

Sewn Bind Off, Fig.3

Step 3: Drop the stitch you sewed through in Step 2. Repeat Steps 1-3 until all stitches have been bound off.

Tutorials   49

STANDARD BIND OFF

Be sure to work this bind off as loosely as possible- a tight cuff is uncomfortable! If you're binding off ribbing, be sure to knit/purl in established pattern.

Standard Bind Off, Fig.1
Step 1: Work 2 stitches.

Standard Bind Off, Fig.2
Step 2: On your right hand needle, take the right stitch and pass it over the left stitch.

Standard Bind Off, Fig.3
Step 3: Work 1 more stitch in pattern. (There should again be 2 stitches on your right hand needle.)

Standard Bind Off, Fig.4
Repeat Steps 2 and 3 until 1 stitch remains, ending with Step 2.

Standard Bind Off, Fig.5
Break yarn, leaving a long (18") tail. Pass tail through the last remaining active stitch.

OTHER TECHNIQUES

KITCHENER STITCH

The Kitchener Stitch is a fantastic way to seamlessly attach two rows of live stitches. For socks, the Kitchener Stitch is mostly used to finish the toes of top down socks, and close up afterthought heels. The Kitchener Stitch can be a little intimidating the first time you try it, but once you get the hang of it, you'll be surprised how satisfying it is!

Kitchener Stitch, Fig.1

Step 1: Hold your sock in your left hand, making sure that your stitches are arranged evenly on two needles, with the points of both needles facing toward the right. Needle 1 is closer to you, and Needle 2 is further away. The "front" of your stitches is the side closest to you and the "back" of your stitches is the side furthest from you, regardless of which needle you are working on. Your long tail should be dangling between the two needles, on the right side of the sock. (If you don't have a long tail, a long piece of scrap yarn can be used instead.) Thread your tail into a yarn needle.

Kitchener Stitch, Fig.2

Step 2: Insert your needle through the front of the first stitch on Needle 1 (knit-wise). Remove this stitch from your knitting needle.

Kitchener Stitch, Fig.3

Step 3: Insert your needle through the back of the next stitch on Needle 1 (purl-wise). Leave this stitch on your knitting needle. Draw yarn through, making the stitch snug but not too tight.

Kitchener Stitch, Fig.4

Step 4: Insert your needle through the back of the first stitch on Needle 2 (purl-wise). Remove this stitch from your knitting needle.

Kitchener Stitch, Fig.5

Step 5: Insert your needle through the front of the next stitch on Needle 2 (knit-wise). Leave this stitch on your knitting needle. Draw yarn through, making the stitch snug but not too tight.

Step 6: Repeat Steps 2-5 until the tail has passed through all your stitches at least once. When complete, break yarn and weave in end.

Note: Frequently check your seam to ensure that the stitches are not too tight and not too loose.

WRAP AND TURN (W&T)

While working W&T's, you will be working back and forth, and will most likely not be working across the whole row, but working short rows instead. These instructions assume you will be working in stockinette stitch.

Right Side Wrap and Turn

Wrap and Turn, Fig.1

Step 1: Knit to desired location as called for in the pattern.

Wrap and Turn, Fig.2

Step 2: Bring yarn to front of knitting.

Wrap and Turn, Fig.3
Step 3: Slip 1 stitch from left to right needle

Wrap and Turn, Fig.4
Step 4: Return yarn to back of knitting, wrapping the yarn around the stitch.

Wrap and Turn, Fig.5
Step 5: Slip wrapped stitch from right to left needle.

Wrap and Turn, Fig.6
Step 6: Turn work, ready to begin a wrong side row.

Wrong Side Wrap and Turn

Wrap and Turn, Fig.7
Steps 1-2: Purl to desired location as called for in the pattern. Bring yarn to back of knitting.

Wrap and Turn, Fig.8
Step 3: Slip 1 stitch from left to right needle.

Tutorials 53

Wrap and Turn, Fig.9
Step 4: Return yarn to front of knitting, wrapping the yarn around the stitch.

Wrap and Turn, Fig.10
Step 5: Slip wrapped stitch from right to left needle.

Wrap and Turn, Fig.11
Step 6: Turn work, ready to begin a right side row.

W&T Gaps
Working W&Ts creates small gaps between otherwise evenly-spaced stitches as they sit on your needle. These gaps will not be seen in the final project, but they can be very helpful guideposts while knitting your socks. A W&T gap is seen to the side of a wrapped stitch, and can be found both on knit and purled rows.

Wrap and Turn Gap (Right Side)

Wrap and Turn Gap (Wrong Side)

Working Wraps

After working W&Ts, you will need to work your wraps with your stitches to avoid holes in your socks.

For a Knit Row

Working Wraps, Fig.1
Step 1: Knit to 1 stitch before the W&T gap. Slip wrapped stitch onto right needle.

Working Wraps, Fig.2
Step 2: With left needle, lift wrap up and onto right needle.

Working Wraps, Fig.3
Step 3: Slip stitch and wrap from right needle back to left needle, separating them as you do.

Working Wraps, Fig.4
Step 4: Knit both the wrap and the stitch together as one (k2tog).

Working Wraps, Fig.5
Step 5: Continue working row as indicated by pattern. If worked correctly, the W&T will be almost invisible.

For a Purl Row

Working Wraps, Fig.6
Step 1: Purl to 1 stitch before W&T gap. Slip wrapped stitch onto right needle.

Working Wraps, Fig.7
Step 2: With left needle, lift wrap up and on to needle.

Working Wraps, Fig.8
Step 3: Slip stitch and wrap on right needle back to left needle, separating them as you do.

Working Wraps, Fig.9
Step 4: Purl both the wrap and the stitch together as one.
Step 5: Continue working row as indicated by pattern. If worked correctly, the W&T will be almost invisible.

FACED CUFF (PICOT & SMOOTH EDGE)

Faced Cuff, Fig.1
Step 1: Turn your sock inside-out. If you used a provisional cast on, remove the CO, transferring all stitches to your needles.

Faced Cuff, Fig.2
Step 2: Fold the cuff toward the inside of the sock along the fold round.

Faced Cuff, Fig.3

Step 3: Use the long tail and a yarn needle to sew each active stitch to a purl bump directly below it, being sure to keep your stitches slightly loose and invisible from the outside (Figures 3-4).

AFTERTHOUGHT HEEL

Afterthought Heel, Fig.1

Step 1: After completing the sock, locate your contrast yarn holding your stitches.

Afterthought Heel, Fig.2

Step 2: Remove scarp yarn, carefullly cutting scrap yarn if desired (*Note:* Do not cut sock yarn!) (Figures 2-3).

Afterthought Heel, Fig.3

Afterthought Heel, Fig.4

Step 3: Pick up live sitches as you go with 2 needles.

Tutorials

Afterthought Heel, Fig. 5

Step 4: Divide your stitches evenly onto 4 needles, being sure you have an even number of stitches on each needle. Continue to work heel.

Stockinette Stitch Pattern, Turned Heel, & Standard Toe in Dandelion

Oddball Stripes Stitch Pattern, Standard Toe, & Afterthought Heel in White, Dandelion, & Electric Blue

Openwork Stripes Stitch Pattern, Standard Toe, & Turned Heel in Electric Blue

NOTES

I love giving socks as gifts to friends and family, but I hate having to give away my plans by asking them to let me measure their feet! Whenever you measure someone's feet, make a note of their size so you don't have to bug them again.

Name: _____

Shoe Size: _____

Foot Diameter: _____

Foot Length: _____

Name: _____

Shoe Size: _____

Foot Diameter: _____

Foot Length: _____

Name: _____

Shoe Size: _____

Foot Diameter: _____

Foot Length: _____

Name: _____

Shoe Size: _____

Foot Diameter: _____

Foot Length: _____

Name: _____

Shoe Size: _____

Foot Diameter: _____

Foot Length: _____

Name: _____

Shoe Size: _____

Foot Diameter: _____

Foot Length: _____

Name: _____

Shoe Size: _____

Foot Diameter: _____

Foot Length: _____

Name: _____

Shoe Size: _____

Foot Diameter: _____

Foot Length: _____

Tiny Dots Stitch Pattern & Standard Toe in White

Oddball Stripes Stitch Pattern, Standard Toe, & Afterthought Heel in White, Dandelion, & Electric Blue

Twin Cable Stitch Pattern, Standard Toe, and Reinforced Heel in Pucker

SOCK SIZE CHART & ABBREVIATIONS

STITCH COUNT CHART

A (sts)	B (sts)	C (sts)	D (sts)	E (sts)
24	12	6	34	2
28	14	7	40	3
32	16	8	46	4
36	18	9	50	4
40	20	10	56	5
44	22	11	62	6
48	24	12	66	6
52	26	13	72	7
56	28	14	78	8
60	30	15	82	8
64	32	16	88	9
68	34	17	94	10
72	36	18	98	10
76	36	19	104	11
80	40	20	110	12
84	42	21	114	12
88	44	22	120	13
92	46	23	126	14
96	48	24	130	14
100	50	25	136	15
104	52	26	142	16
108	54	27	146	16
112	56	28	152	17
116	58	29	158	18
120	60	30	162	18
124	62	31	168	19

ABBREVIATIONS

BO	bind off	M1	make one stitch	RH	right hand	TFL	through front loop
cn	cable needle	M1L	make one left-leaning stitch	rnd(s)	round(s)	tog	together
CC	contrast color			RS	right side	W&T	wrap & turn (see specific instructions in pattern)
CDD	centered double dec	M1R	make one right-leaning stitch	Sk	skip		
CO	cast on			Sk2p	sl 1, k2tog, pass slipped stitch over k2tog: 2 sts dec	WE	work even
cont	continue	MC	main color			WS	wrong side
dec	decrease(es)	P	purl			WYIB	with yarn in back
DPN(s)	double pointed needle(s)	P2tog	purl 2 sts together	SKP	sl, k, psso: 1 st dec	WYIF	with yarn in front
		PM	place marker	SL	slip	YO	yarn over
EOR	every other row	PFB	purl into the front and back of stitch	SM	slip marker		
inc	increase			SSK	sl, sl, k these 2 sts tog		
K	knit	PSSO	pass slipped stitch over	SSP	sl, sl, p these 2 sts tog tbl		
K2tog	knit two sts together						
KFB	knit into the front and back of stitch	PU	pick up	SSSK	sl, sl, sl, k these 3 sts tog		
		P-wise	purlwise	St st	stockinette stitch		
K-wise	knitwise	rep	repeat	sts	stitch(es)		
LH	left hand	Rev St st	reverse stockinette stitch	TBL	through back loop		
M	marker						

SOCK SIZE CHART

		Children's				Women's				Men's					
	US Shoe Size	0-4	4-8	7-11	10-2	3-6	6-9	8-12		6-8	8.5-10	10.5-12	12-13	13-14	
	Length (in inches)	4		5	6	7.5	9	10	11	9.5	10.5	11	11.5	12	
	Circumference (in inches)	4.5	5	5.5	6	6.5	7	7.5	8	8.5	9	9.5	10	10.5	11	11.5	12	12.5	13	13.5	14
Gauge	6	24	28	32	36	36	40	44	48	48	52	56	60	60	64	64	72	72	76	80	84
	6.5	28	32	32	36	40	44	48	52	52	56	60	64	68	68	72	76	80	84	84	88
	7	30	32	36	40	44	48	52	56	56	60	64	68	72	76	80	84	84	88	92	96
	7.5	30	36	40	44	48	52	56	60	60	64	68	72	76	80	84	88	92	96	100	104
	8	36	40	44	48	52	56	60	64	68	72	76	80	84	88	92	96	100	104	108	112
	8.5	36	40	44	48	52	56	60	68	72	76	80	84	88	92	96	100	104	108	112	116
	9	40	44	48	48	56	60	64	72	76	80	84	88	92	96	100	108	112	116	120	124

Knit Picks yarn is both luxe and affordable—a seeming contradiction trounced! But it's not just about the pretty colors; we also care deeply about fiber quality and fair labor practices, leaving you with a gorgeously reliable product you'll turn to time and time again.

THIS COLLECTION FEATURES

Stroll Sock Yarn
Fingering Weight
75% Superwash Merino Wool, 25% Nylon

View these beautiful yarns and more at www.KnitPicks.com

For pattern support, contact customerservice@knitpicks.com